LOVE

Is in the AIR

To my wonderful editor, Alyson Heller, for helping me

tell the story of these amazing women

—D. R.

To Darlie, my bravest little hero

—V. M.

ALADDIN • An imprint of Simon & Schuster Children's Publishing Division • 1230 Avenue of the Americas, New York, New York 10020 • First Aladdin hardcover edition September 2023 • Text copyright © 2023 by Deanna Romito • Illustrations copyright © 2023 by Vivian Mineker • All rights reserved, including the right of reproduction in whole or in part in any form. • ALADDIN and related logo are registered trademarks of Simon & Schuster, Inc. • For information about special discounts for bulk purchases, please contact Simon & Schuster Special Sales at 1-866-506-1949 or business@simonandschuster.com. • The Simon & Schuster Speakers Bureau can bring authors to your live event. For more information or to book an event, contact the Simon & Schuster Speakers Bureau at 1-866-248-3049 or visit our website at www.simonspeakers.com. • Designed by Laura Lyn DiSiena • The illustrations for this book were rendered digitally. • The text of this book was set in Intro. • Manufactured in China 0523 SCP • 2 4 6 8 10 9 7 5 3 1 • Library of Congress Cataloging-in-Publication Data • Names: Romito, Dee, author. | Mineker, Vivian, illustrator. • Title: Love is in the air : the story of aviation pioneer Nancy Harkness Love / by Dee Romito ; illustrated by Vivian Mineker. • Other titles: Story of aviation pioneer Nancy Harkness Love • Description: First Aladdin hardcover edition. | New York : Aladdin, 2023. | Includes bibliographical references. | Audience: Ages 4 to 8 | Summary: "A picture book biography about Nancy Harkness Love, the first female to serve for the Army Air Force and instrumental in founding the Women's Airforce Service Pilots (WASPS) in World War II. Perfect for readers of *Fly Girl, Fly!: Shaesta Waiz Soars Around the World, Herstory* or *Fearless Flyer: Ruth Law and Her Flying Machine*"—Provided by publisher. • Identifiers: LCCN 2022043970 (print) | LCCN 2022043971 (ebook) | ISBN 9781534484191 (hc) | ISBN 9781534484207 (ebook) • Subjects: LCSH: Love, Nancy Harkness, 1914-1976–Juvenile literature. | Women Airforce Service Pilots (U.S.)–Biography–Juvenile literature. | United States. Army Air Forces. Air Transport Command. Ferrying Division–Biography–Juvenile literature. | World War, 1939-1945–Aerial operations, American–Juvenile literature. | World War, 1939-1945–Transportation–United States–Juvenile literature. | United States. Army Air Forces–Transportation–Juvenile literature. | Women air pilots–United States–Biography–Juvenile literature. | Air pilots–United States–Biography–Juvenile literature. • Classification: LCC D790.5.L68 R66 2023 (print) | LCC D790.5.L68 (ebook) | DDC 940.54/4973092 [B]–dc23/eng/20220915 • LC record available at https://lccn.loc.gov/2022043970 • LC ebook record available at https://lccn.loc.gov/2022043971

LOVE
Is in the AIR

~ THE STORY OF ~
AVIATION PIONEER
NANCY HARKNESS LOVE

BY Dee Romito   ILLUSTRATED BY Vivian Mineker

ALADDIN
New York   London   Toronto   Sydney   New Delhi

Young Nancy Harkness loved adventure and had a big imagination. She knew that girls could do anything they dreamed of.

When she was sixteen years old, a barnstormer pilot buzzed through her small town in northern Michigan, giving airplane rides for a penny a pound.

Imagine that!

You paid what you weighed for a ride in an airplane.

Nancy went right over and paid that pilot for a ride.

And she loved it!

Rolls and loops!

Twirls and thrills!

Nancy was in the air.

That day she made a decision that (little did she know) would change the course of history.

She would learn to fly.

There was just one problem. . . .

Her parents wanted her to concentrate on school, not flying.

A determined Nancy made a deal and promised she'd focus on both.

Nancy concentrated hard and learned fast.

Just a few months after her first lesson, she became **one of only two hundred American women** with a private pilot's license.

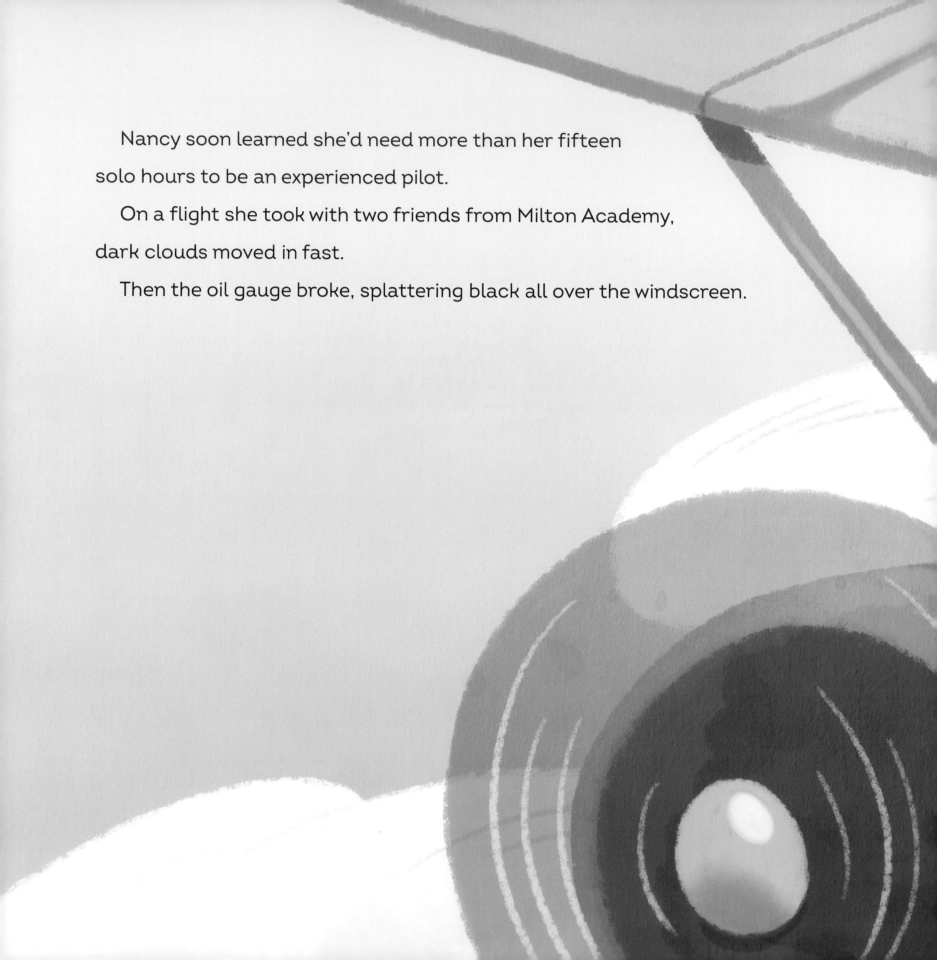

Nancy soon learned she'd need more than her fifteen solo hours to be an experienced pilot.

On a flight she took with two friends from Milton Academy, dark clouds moved in fast.

Then the oil gauge broke, splattering black all over the windscreen.

She had to hang her head out the side window to see!

Nancy spotted an open field below and

landed, avoiding disaster.

Another close call came when her brother, Bob, dared her to fly low and buzz the nearby boys' prep school.

She nearly hit the bell tower!

But Nancy managed to avoid a suspension for her antics. Because even though students at Milton Academy couldn't drive cars, there were no rules about flying planes.

When Nancy went to college, she started an aviation club, earned her commercial pilot's license, and became known as "The Flying Freshman." She also earned her transport license and made extra money flying passengers from one location to another.

Studying French,

but dreaming of flight.

Nancy was in the air.

Unfortunately, people were going through a difficult time called the Great Depression, and Nancy's family couldn't afford to pay her tuition. Nancy was more than halfway through college when she had to drop out.

Several months later, on a mission to make her dream come true, she traveled to Boston to search for a job.

Bob Love hired her to demonstrate airplanes to potential customers. At the time people figured that if a woman could fly one, it couldn't be that hard.

Nancy knew better.

Her flying career was taking off, and soon Nancy and Bob
fell in love and got engaged.

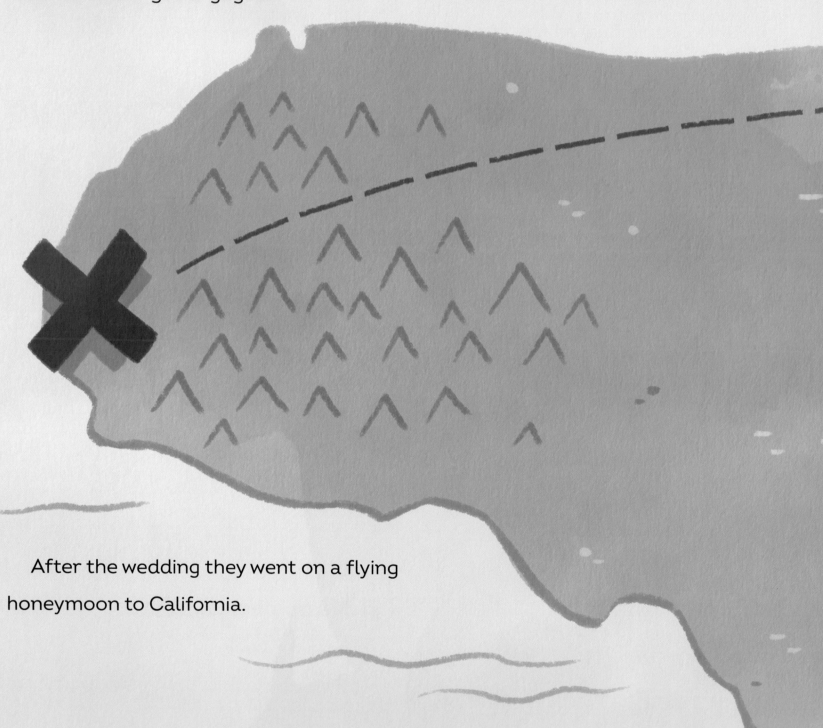

After the wedding they went on a flying
honeymoon to California.

Flying west,

flying high.

Nancy *Love* was in the air.

Nancy's skills were in demand.

She worked for Inter City Aviation,

for the Bureau of Air Commerce,

for the Gwinn Aircar Company.

All before she was
twenty-four years old!

But she wasn't done yet.

Nancy saw a way to help her country: women could ferry airplanes for the US Army Air Corps!

She sent them a letter, but her idea was ultimately turned down.

However . . . by September 1942 the United States had been fighting in World War II for nine months and many men had been lost. The Ferrying Division was in desperate need of pilots to fly military planes from one location to another. Nancy worked with the colonel in charge and their plan was approved.

Female pilots would be allowed to serve in noncombat flying roles—for the first time in US history! And Nancy would lead the group as squadron commander.

NEWS
¢10

Nancy Harkness Love
New WAFS' Boss

"There are probably no more than a hundred women in the country who have all the necessary qualifications," said Nancy.

Only twenty-eight of those women were available and willing to join the new Women's Auxiliary Ferrying Squadron, known as WAFS.

Those twenty-eight women trained twelve hours a day. They were skilled pilots and worked hard, but they often faced resistance and discrimination.

Train, fly, earn respect.

Love was in the air.

Nancy's program merged with another training program, and together they became the Women Airforce Service Pilots, known as WASP.

The women flew all types of military aircraft and took on whatever jobs they were needed for, including teaching male pilots and towing aerial targets.

They delivered more than twelve thousand military planes and flew more than sixty million miles!

BETTY GILLIES

CORNELIA FORT

BARBARA "BJ" ERICKSON

TERESA JAMES

NANCY BATSON

But things were changing.

The United States needed fewer men in the air for fighting,
and the men wanted the ferrying duties back.

Congress voted against making the WASP an official part of the military, which would have given them the benefits and status they deserved.

The program was shut down, and the women were sent home.

After the war ended, Nancy and Bob were both awarded medals for their service to the country.

And though Nancy didn't live to see it happen, close to thirty-five years after the program had begun, the WASP members were finally granted veteran status.

And almost seventy years after these women took flight for their country, the daring female pilots received the highest honor that can be given to private citizens: the Congressional Gold Medal.

Believed, persisted,

made her mark.

Love was in the air.

Nancy Harkness Love went after her dreams despite the many obstacles in her path, paving the way for other female pilots to soar through the skies.

Perhaps it was meant to be that a very special baby, born on Valentine's Day in 1914, would someday have the last name Love. Nancy's official birth name was Hannah Lincoln Harkness, because Nancy's mother wanted to carry on a family tradition. Nancy's father did not. He eventually agreed, but perhaps in protest, he called her Nancy, and so did everyone else.

When Nancy was thirteen, she was touring Europe with her family and witnessed Charles Lindbergh land the *Spirit of St. Louis* in Paris. It was the first successful solo flight over the Atlantic Ocean! But Nancy later said, "You can't make an interesting story out of that, however, it didn't inspire me with an overwhelming desire to fly, as it probably should have!"

Colonel William H. Tunner finally set the plan for the WAFS in motion when he learned of Nancy's skills over the watercooler at work one day. Bob told him that his wife flew back and forth to work and Colonel Tunner exclaimed, "Good Lord, I'm combing the woods for pilots, and here's one right under my nose. Are there many more women like your wife?"

Nancy's first flight in US military aircraft was in a PT-19 on September 7, 1942.

The twenty-eight recruits of the WAFS were later called "The Originals." One of the Originals was Cornelia Fort, who was giving a flying lesson in Hawaii when she saw a Japanese military plane and then witnessed the bombing of Pearl Harbor. Cornelia joined the WAFS and was the first female pilot to die for her country. Another Original was Teresa James, a barnstormer pilot known for her 26-turn spin, who left on a trip that was supposed to take one day and ended up being gone thirty days with only the clothes she had on when she left.

Like Nancy, Jackie Cochran had also pushed for female pilots to fly in the military. When Jackie's plan was not accepted, she took a group of American female pilots to ferry planes for

England. Eventually, Jackie became the leader of the WASP, with Nancy in charge of the women of the ferrying division.

A total of 1,102 female pilots made up the WASP program, and 38 died in the line of duty. While there weren't many women of color in the WASP, it's notable that Hazel Ying Lee became the first Chinese American woman to fly for the US military and Ola Mildred Rexroat was the only Native American woman to serve as a WASP.

I can fill my cup of dreams

When silver springs are far.

If I can find a firefly,

I can reach a star.

Even I, by wishing,

Can wear the Magic shoon,

Even, I, by dreaming,

Can reach up for the Moon.

—HANNAH L. HARKNESS,
Milton Academy *Magus*, December 1929

LEFT: Nancy Love in the cockpit of a Fairchild PT-19A, a training aircraft used by the US Army Air Corps during WWII. The "PT" stands for "Primary Trainer."

RIGHT: Nancy Love (left) and Betty Gillies (right). Gillies was the first pilot to qualify for the WAFS. She and Nancy became the first female pilots to fly the Boeing B-17 Flying Fortress. →

↑ ABOVE: Nancy Love in the cockpit of a B-17 named *Queen Bee*.

RIGHT: Nancy Harkness Love, director of the Women's Auxiliary Ferrying Squadron. →

~ SOURCES ~

A SPECIAL THANK-YOU TO WASP AUTHOR AND HISTORIAN SARAH BYRN RICKMAN FOR HER GUIDANCE AND INSIGHT. AND TO THE LIBRARIANS AT THE LIBRARY OF CONGRESS, WHO ARE ALWAYS SUCH AN AMAZING RESOURCE!

Douglas, Deborah G. "Nancy Harkness Love: Female Pilot and First to Fly for the U.S. Military." Historynet, June 12, 2006. https://www.historynet.com/nancy-harkness-love-female-pilot-and-first-to-fly-for-the-us-military/.

Douglas, Deborah G. "United States Women in Aviation, 1940-1985." Smithsonian Studies in Air and Space. Washington, DC: Smithsonian Institution Press, 1990.

Eads, Jane. "Mrs. Nancy Harkness Love, WAFS' Boss a 'Natural.'" *Courier-Journal*, September 17, 1942.

Eder, Mari K. *The Girls Who Stepped Out of Line*. Naperville, IL: Sourcebooks, 2021.

Gant, Kelli. "Women Involved in Aviation." Ninety-Nines. Accessed March 30, 2018. https://www.ninety-nines.org/women-in-aviation-article.htm.

Ladevich, Laurel, dir. *Fly Girls* (film). For *American Experience* on PBS. Silverlining Productions, May 1999.

Landdeck, Katherine Sharp. *The Women with Silver Wings*. New York: Crown, 2020.

Love, Nancy H. Nancy H. Love to Harry P. Kelliher, December 14, 1937. Smithsonian National Air and Space Museum, Nancy Harkness Love Collection, 1936-1976.

Love, Nancy H. Nancy H. Love to J.C. Bradford, May 24, 1955. Smithsonian National Air and Space Museum, Nancy Harkness Love Collection, 1936-1976.

"Nancy Harkness Love." Vassar Encyclopedia. Accessed March 29, 2018. https://vcencyclopedia.vassar.edu/alumni/nancy-love.html.

Pearson, P. O'Connell. *Fly Girls: The Daring American Women Pilots Who Helped Win WWII*. New York: Simon & Schuster Books for Young Readers, 2018.

Rickman, Sarah Byrn. *Nancy Love and the WASP Ferry Pilots of World War II*. Denton, TX: University of North Texas Press, 2008.

Rickman, Sarah Byrn. *Nancy Love: WASP Pilot*. Palmer Lake, CO: Filter Press, 2019.

Schisgall, Oscar. "The Girls Deliver the Goods." *Baltimore Sun*, February 28, 1943.